SPOTLIGHT ON AMERICAN HISTORY

The Expansion of the United States

Florida, Alaska, Gadsden Purchase, and Mexican Cession

Joseph Stanley

PowerKiDS press™

New York

Published in 2017 by The Rosen Publishing Group, Inc.
29 East 21st Street, New York, NY 10010

Book Design: Samantha DeMartin
Editor: Katie Kawa

Photo Credits: Cover Ed Vebell/Archive Photos/Getty Images; p. 5 https://commons.wikimedia.org/wiki/File:Louisiana1804a.jpg; p. 6 UniversalImagesGroup/Universal Images Group/Getty Images; p. 7 Stock Montage/Archive Photos/Getty Images; p. 9 Universal History Archive/Universal Images Group/Getty Images; p. 10 https://commons.wikimedia.org/wiki/File:American_Progress_(1872)_by_John_Gast.jpg; p. 11 https://commons.wikimedia.org/wiki/File:Map_of_Mexico_1847.jpg; p. 13 https://commons.wikimedia.org/wiki/File:Henry_Clay_Senate3.jpg; p. 14 Witold Skrypczak/Lonely Planet Images/Getty Images; p. 15 Kean Collection/Archive Photos/Getty Images; p. 16 mffoto/Shutterstock.com; p. 17 Pictorial Parade/Archive Photos/Getty Images; p. 18 Hulton Archive/Getty Images; p. 19 https://commons.wikimedia.org/wiki/File:Nome_1900.jpg; p. 20 https://commons.wikimedia.org/wiki/File:Seminole_War_in_Everglades.jpg; p. 21 MPI/Archive Photos/Getty Images.

Library of Congress Cataloging-in-Publication Data

Names: Stanley, Joseph, author.
Title: The expansion of the United States: Florida, Alaska, Gadsden Purchase, and Mexican Cession / Joseph Stanley.
Description: New York : PowerKids Press, 2017. | Series: Spotlight on American history | Includes index.
Identifiers: LCCN 2015050556 | ISBN 9781508149552 (pbk.) | ISBN 9781508149415 (library bound) | ISBN 9781508149200 (6 pack)
Subjects: LCSH: United States--Territorial expansion--Juvenile literature. | Manifest Destiny.
Classification: LCC E179.5 .S77 2017 | DDC 973.3--dc23
LC record available at http://lccn.loc.gov/2015050556

Manufactured in the United States of America

CPSIA Compliance Information: Batch #BS16PK: For further information contact Rosen Publishing, New York, New York at 1-800-237-9932.

CONTENTS

A GROWING NATION

The United States is one of the largest countries in the world. It stretches from the Atlantic Ocean to the Pacific Ocean and also includes the states of Alaska and Hawaii. However, the United States wasn't always the size it is today. It was once only a narrow strip of 13 states along the coast of the Atlantic Ocean.

How did the United States grow to cover the area it does now? A series of purchases and treaties during the 1800s expanded the nation quickly. In less than 100 years, the United States grew from its original size to reach from one ocean to another.

The first major step on the path of expansion came in 1803. That year, U.S. President Thomas Jefferson purchased the Louisiana Territory from France. The United States gained lands from the Mississippi River to the Rocky Mountains, nearly doubling the country's size. Expansion continued at a rapid rate after the Louisiana Purchase.

The Louisiana Purchase was the beginning of the expansion of the United States. After this land deal was completed, Americans began to look south, west, and even north to find new lands to settle. They came to believe in the idea of Manifest ***Destiny****, which was the belief that the United States was meant to reach from the Atlantic Ocean to the Pacific Ocean.*

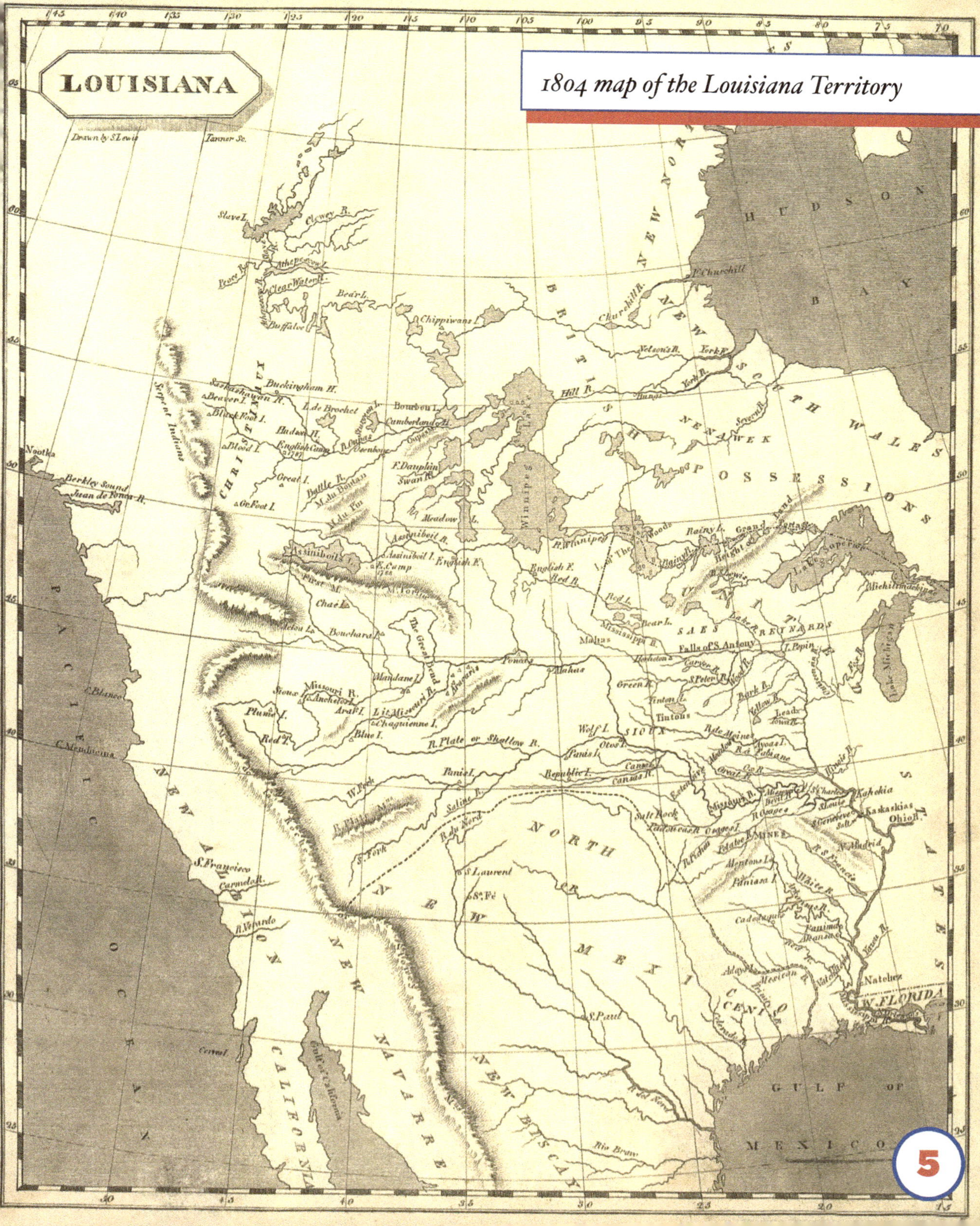

1804 map of the Louisiana Territory

FLORIDA JOINS THE UNITED STATES

After the Louisiana Purchase, U.S. leaders turned their attention to Florida, which was a Spanish colony at the time. Spain had controlled Florida since the 1500s, but Britain took over the colony in 1763, splitting it into East Florida and West Florida. Twenty years later, Spain regained control of both halves of Florida.

Military leader and future president Andrew Jackson, shown here, led ***raids*** *against Native Americans in Florida before the signing of the Adams-Onís Treaty. His presence in Florida helped bring about the* ***acquisition*** *of that land for the United States.*

In 1810, citizens of West Florida **rebelled** against Spain. The United States claimed a portion of West Florida was part of the Louisiana Territory it now owned, and years of border **disputes** followed.

The entire area now known as Florida became part of the United States in 1819 with the signing of the Adams-Onís Treaty. This treaty was named after U.S. Secretary of State John Quincy Adams and Spanish minister Luis de Onís. This treaty—also known as the Transcontinental Treaty—wasn't ratified, or formally approved, until 1821. Florida officially became a U.S. state in 1845.

John Quincy Adams

EXPANSION LEADS TO WAR

The United States continued to expand throughout the first half of the 1800s. U.S. leaders agreed to a joint occupation of **Oregon Country** with Britain in 1818, and the border between those two countries' lands in the region was officially set in 1846.

The United States also **annexed** Texas. When Texas became part of the United States in 1845, a bitter border dispute with Mexico began. U.S. leaders claimed the border between Texas and Mexico was the Rio Grande. Mexican leaders, however, claimed the Nueces River was the border. U.S. leaders didn't want to set the border at the Nueces River because that would give more land to Mexico.

Soon after Texas was annexed, U.S. President James K. Polk sent troops under the command of General Zachary Taylor to the Rio Grande. On April 25, 1846, fighting broke out between those troops and Mexican forces, marking the start of the U.S.-Mexican War.

The U.S.-Mexican War was a turning point in the push to expand the United States from the Atlantic Ocean to the Pacific Ocean. Shown here is an image of the Battle of Monterrey, which was a major battle in this war.

THE MEXICAN CESSION

The United States won battle after battle in the U.S.-Mexican War. In September 1847, U.S. troops marched into Mexico City, which marked the end of armed conflict. However, it took months for the two countries to **negotiate** a treaty. Finally, on February 2, 1848, the Treaty of Guadalupe Hidalgo was signed.

The Treaty of Guadalupe Hidalgo officially ended the U.S.-Mexican War. It also granted the

By the time the Treaty of Guadalupe Hidalgo was signed, the United States had realized the dream of Manifest Destiny. The concept of Manifest Destiny was shown through paintings, such as American Progress *by John Gast, shown here.*

Shown here is a map used during treaty negotiations between the United States and Mexico.

United States a large amount of land known as the Mexican Cession. The Mexican Cession included lands in what are now the states of California, Nevada, Utah, New Mexico, Arizona, Wyoming, and Colorado. With this treaty, Mexico also agreed to give up all claims to lands in Texas, and the border between Texas and Mexico was set at the Rio Grande.

In exchange for these new lands, the United States paid Mexico $15 million. It also promised to pay back **debts** Mexico owed to U.S. citizens.

REACHING A COMPROMISE

The Mexican Cession became part of the United States during a difficult time in the nation's history. Debates over the issue of slavery—especially slavery in new territories—were reaching a boiling point.

Before the end of the U.S.-Mexican War, David Wilmot, who was a member of Congress from Pennsylvania, proposed that slavery shouldn't be allowed in any territories the United States acquired after the war was over. This became known as the Wilmot Proviso.

Since the Wilmot Proviso never became a law, the question of whether or not to allow slavery in the lands of the Mexican Cession remained. The Compromise of 1850 attempted to address some of these concerns. This set of five laws proposed by Henry Clay allowed California to enter the Union as a free state and officially recognized Utah and New Mexico as territories. It ended the slave trade in what's now Washington, D.C. However, it also allowed for the passage of a more severe **Fugitive Slave Act**.

Senator Henry Clay of Kentucky, shown here, proposed the Compromise of 1850. He's sometimes called "the Great Compromiser."

MORE MEXICAN LANDS

While the Treaty of Guadalupe Hidalgo ended the war between the United States and Mexico, **tensions** remained high between the two countries into the 1850s. Border disputes continued, especially in the area around the Mesilla Valley. Both countries claimed the valley as their own land.

The United States wanted to renegotiate its border with Mexico to acquire more land for a southern railroad route. Americans dreamed of

Mesilla Valley

By the 1850s, railroads were becoming an important way to travel across the rapidly expanding United States. The Southern Pacific Railroad eventually ran through part of the land acquired in the Gadsden Purchase.

creating a railroad that ran from one end of the country to the other, and acquiring more lands from Mexico would help make a southern section of that railroad a reality.

On December 30, 1853, James Gadsden, who was the U.S. minister to Mexico, signed a treaty with Mexican President Antonio de Santa Anna. This treaty, which became known as the Gadsden Purchase, gave the United States land in what's now Arizona and New Mexico for $10 million. With this treaty, the United States expanded by nearly 30,000 square miles (77,700 sq km).

"SEWARD'S FOLLY"

The Gadsden Purchase allowed the United States to continue to expand into new parts of the Southwest. Another major purchase allowed the United States to expand farther north than many Americans ever dreamed of traveling.

Alaska is now a U.S. state, but it was once under the control of Russia. However, Russian interest in Alaska began to decrease by the mid-1800s.

When Alaska was first purchased by the United States, Americans didn't understand the value of this land.

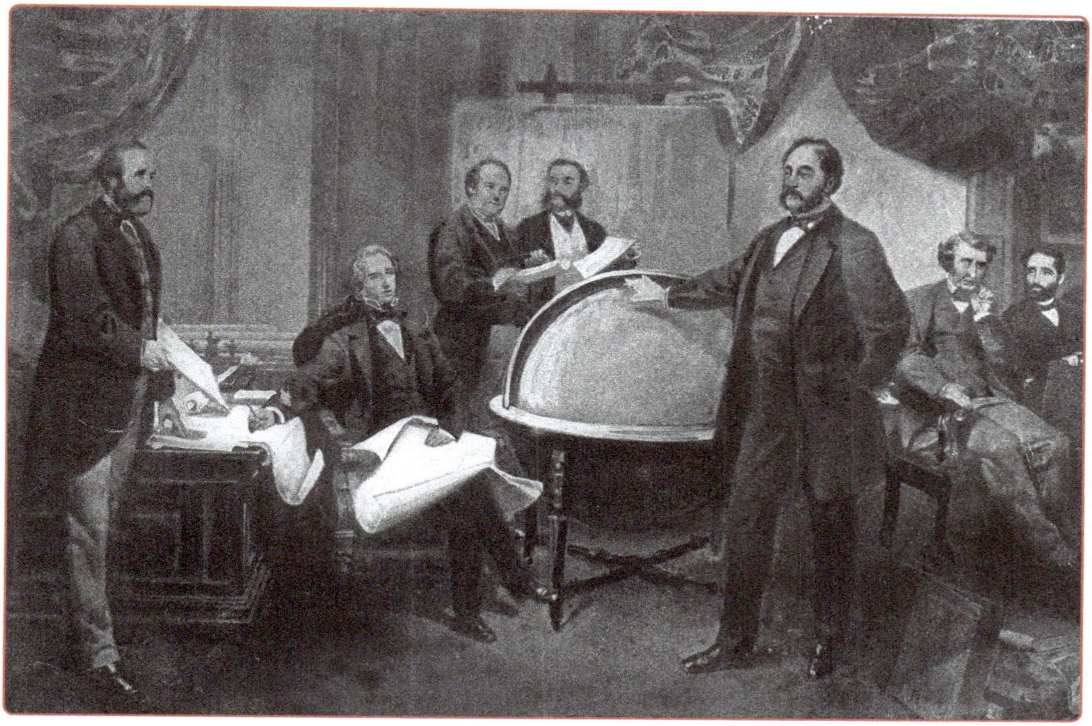

Shown here is an illustration of the signing of the treaty in which the United States agreed to purchase Alaska from Russia.

The time was right for the United States to acquire that land. On March 30, 1867, U.S. Secretary of State William Seward agreed to purchase Alaska from Russia. For $7.2 million, the United States acquired nearly 600,000 square miles (1,553,993 sq km) of land.

Alaska was a piece of land that was largely unexplored, so no one knew what resources it could provide. Many Americans mocked the purchase of this land at first. They called the deal "Seward's **Folly**" and called Alaska "Seward's Icebox."

GOING FOR THE GOLD

At the end of the 19th century, the discovery of gold brought people to Alaska in huge numbers. The purchase of Alaska was no longer seen as a "folly" but as a smart land acquisition.

In August 1896, gold was discovered in Canada's Yukon Territory. Because the gold was found in a **tributary** of the Klondike River, this became known as the Klondike Gold Rush. During the

This photograph shows miners during the Klondike Gold Rush. Thousands of miners like these men passed through or settled in Alaska at the end of the 19th century.

Nome, Alaska, in 1900

Klondike Gold Rush, people stayed in Alaskan towns before traveling to the Yukon Territory. This led to the rapid growth of towns such as Skagway, Alaska.

As the Klondike Gold Rush was winding down, gold was discovered in Nome, Alaska, and a new gold rush began. In 1899, tens of thousands of people flocked to Nome because gold could easily be found on its beaches. Gold was also found a few years later in Fairbanks. Suddenly, Alaska was no longer seen as only icy wilderness. It was a place of resources, riches, and adventure.

THE PRICE OF EXPANSION

Americans believed it was their country's destiny to expand into new lands. However, as the United States expanded, settlers encountered Native American groups who'd been living on those lands for centuries. While the United States gained much during this period of expansion, Native Americans lost much, including their homelands and sometimes their lives.

This image shows U.S. forces searching for Native Americans during the Seminole Wars.

As more settlers came to California looking for gold, they began to fight more frequently with the Native Americans who already lived there.

Between 1817 and 1858, the U.S. government fought a series of wars with the Seminole people of Florida. The Seminole Wars allowed white settlers to take over Seminole lands in Florida.

Another example of Native Americans paying the price for U.S. expansion was found in California. During the California Gold Rush, which began in 1848, thousands of settlers came to this part of the Mexican Cession. Attacks carried out by some of these settlers contributed to a huge decrease in the Native American population in California—from around 150,000 in 1845 to around 30,000 in 1870.

A CENTURY OF GROWTH

The 19th century was a period of major change for the United States. In less than 100 years, it grew from a small group of states into a large and powerful country with lands that reached from Maine to California and Florida to Alaska. To close out this century of expansion, the United States annexed Hawaii in 1898.

The United States expanded in different ways—sometimes by peaceful negotiation and sometimes by violent force. It was often Native Americans who were on the receiving end of that violent force. As the country expanded, Native American lands shrank, until most Native Americans were living on reservations set up by the U.S. government.

As the United States grew in size, it also grew in strength. By the start of the 20th century, other countries were beginning to consider it a world power. The expansion of the United States during the 1800s shaped the country into what it is today—in more ways than one.

GLOSSARY

acquisition (aa-kwuh-ZIH-shun): The act of coming to own something.

annex (AA-nehks): To take over an area and make it part of a larger territory.

debt (DEHT): Money owed to another.

destiny (DEHS-tuh-nee): The things that are meant to happen in the future.

dispute (dih-SPYOOT): A disagreement.

folly (FAH-lee): A foolish act or idea.

Fugitive Slave Act (FYOO-juh-tihv SLAYV AKT): A federal law that allowed for the capture and return of runaway slaves in the United States.

negotiate (nih-GO-shee-ayt): To discuss something formally in order to reach an agreement.

Oregon Country (OHR-ih-guhn KUHN-tree): The name given in the 1800s to the area between the Rocky Mountains and the Pacific Ocean and between what is now northern California and Alaska.

raid (RAYD): A surprise attack on an enemy.

rebel (rih-BEL): To fight against authority.

tension (TEN-chuhn): A state in which people, groups, or countries disagree with and feel anger toward each other.

tributary (TRIB-yuh-tehr-ee): A stream that flows into a larger stream, river, or lake.

INDEX

PRIMARY SOURCE LIST

Page 5: Map of Louisiana Territory. Created by Samuel Lewis. 1804. Engraved map. Originally published in Aaron Arrowsmith's *New and Elegant General Atlas*. Now kept at the Library of Congress, Geography and Map Division, Washington, D.C.

Page 10: *American Progress*. Print, based on original painting created by John Gast. 1872. Original now kept at the Autry Museum of the American West, Los Angeles, California.

Page 11: Map of the United States of Mexico. Created by J. Distrunell. 1847. Now kept at the National Archives, Washington, D.C.

Page 19: Photograph of Nome, Alaska. Creator unknown. 1900. Now kept at the Library of Congress, Prints and Photographs Division, Washington, D.C.

WEBSITES

Due to the changing nature of Internet links, PowerKids Press has developed an online list of websites related to the subject of this book. This site is updated regularly. Please use this link to access the list: www.powerkidslinks.com/soah/expus